The Reduced History of TENNIS

First published in 2006 by
André Deutsch Ltd
An imprint of the
Carlton Publishing Group
20 Mortimer Street
London W1T 3JW

A CIP catalogue record for this book
is available from the British Library

ISBN 10: 0-233-00191-3
ISBN 13: 978-0-233-00191-3

Printed in Singapore

Commissioning Editor: Martin Corteel
Project Art Editor: Darren Jordan
Production: Lisa French

The Reduced History of TENNIS

The story of the genteel racket-and-ball game squeezed into 101 smashes and lobs

Richard Pendleton Illustrations by Tony Husband

ANDRE DEUTSCH

Other titles in the Reduced History series

The Reduced History of Football
ISBN 0-233-00077-1

The Reduced History of Cricket
ISBN 0-233-00126-3

The Reduced History of Golf
ISBN 0-233-00121-2

The Reduced History of Rugby
ISBN 0-233-00122-0

The Reduced History of Britain
ISBN 0-233-00190-5

INTRODUCTION

Tennis. It's a sport that combines the gentility of a vicarage garden party with the brute force of all-in wrestling, a sport whose crisp tennis whites, polite handshakes and watery fruit drinks are at odds with its history of pushy parents, petulant prodigies, enormous egos and lost tempers that have left the courts littered with the bodies of slain kings, queens and even other players.

We've waded through the blood, the gore, the sweaty underwear and the debris of broken dreams to raid the annals of tennis history for some of its juiciest moments, and presented them in this handy, pocket-sized book.

Scientifically proven not to benefit your forehand or help your concentration, and containing no useful instructional diagrams, it will fit nicely into your racket bag and keep your spirits up during those breaks between games, or during those long Wimbledon rain delays when there's a real risk that you could be asked to join in a mass sing-along of the popular hits of yesteryear.

So welcome to *The Reduced History of Tennis*, the only tennis book that takes you from the twelfth century to the twenty-first in the time it takes you to lace up a pair of Dunlop Green Flash trainers …

FIRST SET

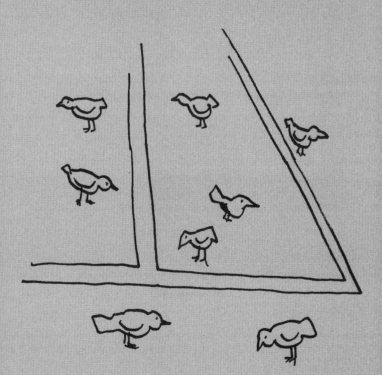

The French connection

Gallic sportsmen serve up some piquant new tennis terms

The French. Their cuisine takes place in an all-garlic environment, their waiters are rude and their toilets lack many basic features, but we have them to thank for the arcane vocabulary of modern tennis.

Getting a sneakily early start by inventing a racketless game known as *jeu de paume*, or "game of palm", in the thirteenth century, French players quickly got to work by giving things names. "Tennis", for instance, comes from *tenez*, a form of the verb which means "to hold", racket from *raquette*, while deuce is thought to be an abbreviation of "*à deux le jeu*", literally "to both the game".

Nobody quite knows how "love" came to refer to zero, but when dealing with a sport that started out under the name "game of palm", it's probably best not to ask too many questions.

Courtside regicide

Uneasy lies the head that wears the crown – and the king that holds a racket

You might expect a king to die on the battlefield – it is, after all, a hazardous place littered with sharp objects. But, with a combination of stupidity and basic bad luck, some monarchs have turned the tennis court, which contains nothing more dangerous than a net, two rackets and a ball, into a veritable arena of death.

In 1316 Louis X of France died after a strenuous game of *jeu de paume*, the early form of tennis. Some say he had a chill, others that he was suffering from dehydration, presumably after ignoring the advice of the Minister for Isotonic Sports Drinks – but then he was known as "Louis the Stubborn" for a reason.

Another French king, Charles VIII, was striding confidently on to the court built into the dry moat at the Château of Amboise, but before his courtiers could shout "don't hit your head on that dangerously low doorway and sustain a fatal injury", he did just that and died several hours later.

Prisoner of tennis

Nobleman doing porridge stirs up English sport

Agincourt may have been a shot in the arm for the English arrow industry, but few people are aware that the wars between England and France were also very good news for the game of tennis. Among the prisoners taken by the English was Prince Charles d'Orléans, scion of the French royal line – and tennis star.

Having spent many years behind bars, Charles was made the responsibility of Sir John Wingfield, who put him up at Wingfield Castle and, under a relaxed regime certain to outrage Tudor newspaper columnists, allowed him to play tennis. The sport was already catching on with the English court, but it was the Wingfield connection that would prove to be important: one of Sir John's descendants was Major Walter Wingfield – who later invented lawn tennis.

Boleyn vs. Tudor

Arguing the toss with King Henry means that it's heads you lose

With a waist that measured 54 inches by the time of his death in 1547, Henry VIII may sound like an unlikely early tennis star, but the portly monarch made a formidable opponent in more ways than one.

Henry helped to popularize real tennis, the forerunner of the modern game. The court he had built at Hampton Court Palace is still in use, and in his younger – and thinner – days, the king was also a useful player. One adoring spectator remembered his "fair skin glowing through his shirt", but for all Henry's enthusiasm, the game doesn't seem to have improved his temper.

He had his second wife, Anne Boleyn, arrested for treason while she was watching tennis in Greenwich, and legend has it that he was playing tennis at the time she was executed. Anne Boleyn's fondness for real tennis is commemorated by a tournament in the US known as the Anne Boleyn Memorial Handicap, which just goes to show that in tennis, losing your head is no bar to immortality.

5 Tennis gets real

Peasants storm the barricades as tennis shuts itself inside

Played with wooden rackets in a walled court with a covered walkway running round three sides to complicated, centuries-old rules, real tennis looks oddly like a two-sided game of squash being played in a cramped hotel lobby. But this is the great-granddad of modern tennis and the oldest of all the racket sports.

The "real" in the name was another way of writing "royal", because it first became popular, during the sixteenth century, with the royal families of Europe, as they were the only people who weren't too busy suffering the ravages of famine or dying of the bubonic plague to find time to practise their forehand.

By the eighteenth century, society had changed. Plague and hunger had been joined by revolution as the favourite pastimes of the peasantry, with the result that most of the aristocratic real tennis players had other things on their minds – like making a real effort to

avoid being lynched by angry mobs.

Real tennis went into decline, but it was edging back into fashion just in time to be dealt a final blow to the head by the arrival of lawn tennis. Suddenly, you didn't need a large indoor court or a degree-level understanding of the rules to play tennis. All you needed was a lawn, some basic equipment and an ability to remember whose turn it was to serve.

Faced with this blatant appeal to populism, real tennis did what it did best and went into decline. Again. It's still played today, although you're unlikely to see many games being televised, and if you're thinking about trying it for yourself, you may need a road atlas as there are just under 30 courts around Britain.

You might also find it difficult to borrow a suitable racket. Few companies still make them as they have to be made of wood by specially trained craftsmen and the frame alone could cost you at least £100 – a right royal sum.

Baroque and roll

Tantrum costs turbulent tennis-playing artist his day in court

To look upon Caravaggio's greatest works is to look upon the full savagery and glory of the human condition, but to dispute the score of a game of tennis with him was to take your life in your hands, as Ranuccio Tomassoni found out to his cost in May 1606.

The temperamental Baroque artist was as handy with a racket as he was with a brush, but when Tomassoni made the mistake of saying that he found his interpretation of the score to be unduly creative, Caravaggio reached for his sword instead. Seconds later, his opponent was dead, Caravaggio was severely injured and Italian editors had news for the front pages, the back pages and the Saturday arts supplement.

Caravaggio died four years later, shortly before the arrival of a pardon for the murder. His death may have been bad news for Baroque, but Italian tennis players and art critics could have been forgiven for breathing a sigh of relief.

Tennis goes clubbing

Suburban spa town stars set up an early rival to SW17

Move over Wimbledon: Leamington Spa is the true spiritual home of tennis. This is where the first lawn tennis club was formed in 1872 by an unlikely combination of a major, a Spaniard and two doctors.

Major Henry Gem and Baptista Pereira were already used to playing the Spanish ball game *pelota* when they moved to Leamington and began a regular fixture with two doctors from the local hospital. *Pelota* gave way to lawn tennis, and the Leamington Tennis Club was formed in 1872 on a lawn behind the Manor House Hotel.

It's still going strong today, although, inexplicably, Wimbledon seems to get all the attention.

Branding consultants charge millions for their expertise, but back in 1874 when Major Walter Wingfield was trying to think up a name for his new ball game, branding was something you did to cattle and people had real jobs, so the major had to seek inspiration elsewhere.

He came up with Sphairistike, after the Greek for "ball game", but it didn't last long. It's rumoured that he was annoyed by people abbreviating it to "Sticky", and the name quickly gave way to something more recognizable – lawn tennis. Which is probably just as well, as it's hard to imagine Federer or Agassi competing for the honour of being Stickiest.

Mustachioed maestro

Opulent facial hair puts Beckenham boy on the map

If there's one thing that the modern game lacks, it's moustaches. John Newcombe had the last truly great 'tache in tennis, a defiantly irony-free creation that even the biker out of the Village People would have admired. But to find the definitive tennis player's moustache, you have to go back to 1885 when Tom Pettitt became world real tennis champion.

Tom Pettitt was born in Beckenham and emigrated to Boston, where he found a job as a dressing-room attendant at a prestigious private real tennis court. Being an industrious type, young Pettitt applied himself as zealously with the racket as he did with the towels, and quickly became the club pro.

He was world champion for five years before becoming a full-time coach. He was also one of the first lawn tennis players – he started playing in 1876 – and once used a champagne bottle as a bat. But it's for his magnificent moustache that he deserves a mention here – and for the fact that, while he may have looked like a walrus, he never played like one.

10 MCC rules. Okay?

Cricket goes into bat when lawlessness stumps tennis

By the late eighteenth century, new versions of tennis were coming out every week. It seemed like any chap with enough time on his hands and a suitably large front garden could invent a new ball game and advertise it to other chaps in the pages of popular publications. These chaps would then modify it and sell the new game to some more chaps, and so, tennis began to breed. Like bacteria.

While this was great news for the health of the nation, except for those hapless unfortunates trampled in the rush to the court, it didn't amuse the MCC, cricket's governing body. In fact, they were outraged by this frankly un-British confusion and finally cried "Enough!" – or, more likely, "Egad!" – in early 1875.

Used to the order and tradition of their own sport, the MCC grabbed the upstart young game by the scruff of the neck, as though it had been caught smoking behind the pavilion, and set about whipping it into shape.

The first stage was to thrash out a single, definitive set of rules, which is exactly what the MCC, having licked its figurative pencil, sat down to do. Fortunately nobody thought to ask them the very reasonable question as to whether it was really any of their business, and on May 24, 1875, the new rules were produced like a particularly simple piece of Latin prep being handed to an idiot child.

Setting the size of the court, the height of the net and the basic principles that governed the service game, the new rules were certainly thorough but, unlike most of the members of the MCC, they weren't destined to last very long before yielding to change. Experience made it necessary to reduce the height of the net and various other adjustments were made in the following years.

The embryonic tennis establishment had barely waited before fiddling with the new rules that they had been given, and, to the sound of wooden net posts across the country being shortened, the MCC retired, harrumphing, back to the sanctuary of the Long Room.

The All England Club

Tennis rolls over croquet in the battle of lawn dominance

Finding itself strapped for cash and in need of a pony-drawn roller to keep its lawns nice and smooth, the All England Croquet Club decided to raise money and accommodate its raffish younger members by holding a tennis tournament. With the club's name duly changed to the All England Lawn Tennis and Croquet Club, the Championships were born.

Not everybody was impressed with the tournament, now known simply as Wimbledon, or even with lawn tennis. At what may well have been the world's first post-match interview, Spencer Gore, winner of the inaugural men's singles event, was heard to remark that "it'll never catch on".

Lottie conquers the world

The first lady of Edwardian sport finds winning a doddle

Back in the days when the world was divided into gentlemen and ladies, amateurs and professionals, Charlotte "Lottie" Dod was the acme of the talented lady amateur and in 1887 she set a record that still stands by becoming the youngest-ever Wimbledon women's singles champion.

Lottie was 15 when she won her first title at the All England Club, and went on to win it another four times before her last competitive season in 1893. She also won gold in the ladies' singles event at the 1904 Olympics, won silver in the archery competition at the 1908 Olympics, played hockey for England and spent her winters skating and tobogganing.

Had Lottie been around now, someone would have been on hand to give her a suitably pithy nickname. As it was, her nickname must have been one of the few disappointments of her career. The best that the gentlemen of the Victorian press could do? "The Little Wonder".

The Cup runneth away
The colourful past of tennis's most wayward trophy

You may never have heard of Rowland Rhodes, but tennis wouldn't be the same without him, because in 1899 the sport's foremost alliterating silversmith was given the job of making the trophy later known to posterity as the Davis Cup.

A knock-out tournament contested by players representing their respective countries, the competition was set up by four players from Harvard University, including Dwight Davis, who bought the trophy and who gave his name to the tournament after his death in 1945. Britain and the USA were the original competitors, but the modern tournament is open to over a hundred countries.

Rhodes also designed a set of cutlery for the White House, but it's unlikely that even the president's spoons had as colourful a career as the Davis Cup. In 1933 the victorious British team took it clubbing around Paris, where the players drank champagne out of it. The Cup is now kept by the International Tennis Federation, and is believed to be teetotal.

The Doherty brothers were the equivalent in Edwardian tennis of the Mitchell brothers, only with more pleasing accents and a fondness for flannels, and 1905 saw them at the end of an era. No, not a badly acted death in a hackneyed soap opera, but the last of their eight Wimbledon doubles titles.

Older brother Reginald Doherty, known as "Big Do", was seen as the weaker of the two, but still managed to become Wimbledon singles champion four times, beating younger brother Laurie in 1898. Laurie, aka "Little Do", won his first title in 1902, and then won a further four in consecutive years, as well as winning the US Championships and taking gold for singles in the 1900 Olympics.

Just like Phil and Grant, they were even more effective as a pair and, as well as their eight Wimbledon doubles titles, they also claimed gold together in the doubles event at the 1900 Olympics. And you can be sure that they loved their old mum. Oh, yes.

15 Foul play

Wimbledon finalist marooned by nasty niff from open and shut case

Some players have a bit of a temper, but not many of them go as far as the 1879 Wimbledon finalist Vere Thomas St Leger Goold. A flamboyant player from County Cork, by 1907 he was living in reduced circumstances and desperately attempting to make a living in the casinos of Monte Carlo.

Just how desperately was revealed when a hotel porter noticed a smell coming from Goold's luggage and contacted police, who found two halves of a woman's body. At the trial it was revealed that Goold and his wife had borrowed money and jewellery from the woman, and then killed her when she tried to reclaim it.

Goold was sent to the Devil's Island penal colony where he died a year later, and his wife, in prison in France, soon followed him. The identity of his Wimbledon opponent way back in 1879 made it all the more surreal: Goold had lost to the Reverend Hartley, making the game a real clash of saint vs. sinner.

Hip flask, hipper attire

Glimpse of stocking shocking, but brandy goes down well

Short of arriving for your first-round game dressed as a giant chicken, it's almost impossible to cause a sensation in modern tennis, but back in 1919 Suzanne Lenglen caused an uproar with nothing more scandalous than bare forearms.

Lenglen's forearms were displayed by the lightweight, ankle-length dresses she wore which favoured her acrobatic style of play. They may have been practical, but this was a time when even uncovered piano legs were seen as unbearably erotic, and in contrast her opponent in the final, Dorothea Chambers, seemed to have turned up dressed for a wedding.

Winning the game effectively won Lenglen the argument, but her daring dresses were not her only secret weapon. During the breaks between games, Lenglen sipped brandy supplied by her father. Suitably fortified, she went on to win five more Wimbledon titles, as corset-makers tore their unsold garments in rage.

17 Roland Garros

Legendary airman's legacy leaves mortals with feet of clay

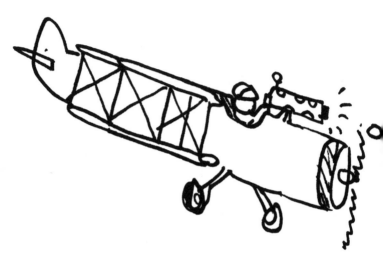

The French Championships used to be a nomadic tournament, wandering between the Racing Club de France and the Stade Français until it settled at its present home, Roland Garros, in 1928. Named after a French airman who died in the First World War, it's jinxed some of the game's greatest players ever since.

Garros had been a member at Stade Français and in 1913 became the first person to fly across the Mediterranean. When war broke out a year later, Roland, being a patriotic sort of chap, put his flying

skills at the disposal of his country and soon became a feared air ace.

His luck let him down when he crashed and was captured, but he escaped and returned to the front line. Then, however, it ran out completely when he crashed again and died. Fast forward 14 years and, after its team won the Davis Cup, France decided that it needed a new venue in which to defend the title the following year. When the new ground was built on land that had belonged to Stade Français, it was duly named after the club's

illustrious former member.

Perhaps Garros does stalk the courts of "his" ground, haunting anyone vain enough to reach for the sky, but a more prosaic answer may be that the new stadium was equipped with red clay courts, making Roland Garros unique among the four Grand Slam venues.

Clay calls on different playing skills to the other tournaments and, to date, the Grand Slam dreams of Lindsay Davenport, Martina Hingis and Roger Federer have all disappeared in a cloud of red dust. Even the otherwise unstoppable Pete Sampras never won there.

Still, it's reassuring to know that the jinx affects French players as well. Yannick Noah was the last winner of the men's singles way back in 1983. When asked about the lack of French champions, he replied: "Everybody knows the French have a problem with winning." Oh la la, Mr Noah…

18 One for all...

Cavalier young blades who cut a dash in twenties tennis

The year is 1927. Lindbergh flies the Atlantic, *The Jazz Singer* introduces sound and breathtakingly casual racism to the cinema, and the world of tennis is shocked and thrilled as the Four Musketeers burst on to the international scene.

This development was not, as you might think, anything to do with a badly misconceived sequel to the Alexandre Dumas classic in which four exotically dressed players did battle with Cardinal Richelieu across the tennis courts of Europe, exchanging forehands and witty repartee ... but it was the next best thing.

The musketeers in this instance were four French tennis players, Jean Borotra, Jacques Brugnon,

Henri Cochet and René Lacoste, and their achievement was to break America's muscular grip on tennis by winning the Davis Cup.

Prior to 1927, the Americans had won the cup seven years in a row, on the last two occasions crushing France 5–0 one year and 4–1 the next – a period of dominance that has still not been bettered. But the French finally gained their revenge in dramatic fashion with a 3–2 win over their hosts in Philadelphia.

America's star singles player, Bill Tilden, suffered a shock four-set defeat to Henri Lacoste in the second leg of his singles match, levelling the score at 2–2 going into the final, deciding singles game between Henri Cochet and Bill Johnston.

Cynics might point out that Bill Johnston was a physical wreck who would retire from competition altogether at the end of the season, but the game still went to four sets before Cochet's fitness won the day. The Gallic foursome proved that the victory had been no fluke by winning a further five Davis Cup titles in consecutive years, although the Davis Cup is just one part of their legacy.

The musketeers were equally effective in singles combat, and won a total of 18 Grand Slam singles titles between them. It just goes to show the truth of the motto "one for all, and all for tennis", ... as the players themselves probably never said.

Moody streak

The poker-faced player who never gave much away

Wimbledon caught its breath at the ladies' singles final in 1933 when Helen Wills Moody dropped a set to her opponent Dorothy Round. It might not sound like the stuff of high drama, as Wills Moody still went on to win, but it brought to an end one of the most remarkable runs of form in the women's game.

Before the final, Wills Moody had gone six years without losing a set, a run that contributed to a career total of eight Wimbledon titles, seven US Championships, four French Championships in singles, and numerous doubles titles.

Not that she seemed particularly pleased. Known as Little Miss Poker Face, Wills Moody met triumph and disaster with the same impassive expression – and then came back the following year and clubbed disaster to death at the back of the court with a meaty forehand.

Wimbledon's barley water

Fruit drink maintains cordial relations with players past and present

Only in Britain would a drink with the name "barley water" be seen as an ideal thirst-quencher. Its name may sound like a euphemism for something much less desirable, but Robinson's finest has been a fixture of Wimbledon ever since it was created in the men's changing rooms and first served at the Championships in 1935.

Robinson's has occupied its reassuring position by the umpire's chair ever since, proving that you don't need a catchy name to be popular. With 5,400 Robinson's drinks drunk every second, the message from the tennis lawns of Britain is clear: keep your sugary American soft drinks with silly names and enough additives to keep a class of five-year-olds awake for three weeks, we're sticking with our barley water. And no, we don't want to supersize it, either. Go away.

Fred gets shirty

Britain's last Wimbledon winner drops his pipe and becomes an icon

Fred Perry won the last of his three Wimbledon titles in 1936, a fact often dusted off and used to crush British players under the weight of national expectation, so it might be better for the mental health of the country's rising tennis stars to concentrate on the other part of the Fred Perry legacy – the polo shirt.

The company started out by making sweatbands, only introducing the polo shirt in 1952, and although it was an instant success, choosing the distinctive laurel wreath logo had taken a while longer. The wreath, a symbol of Perry's many triumphs, might seem the obvious choice now, but at the time his business partner had to talk him out of his first idea – a silhouette of a pipe.

The mysterious Mr G

Sweden's crowning glory serves up a smorgasbord of tennis talent

Over 60 years before Ali G burst on the scene with a cheery "booyakasha", his namesake Mr G bigged up European tennis in 1936 by starting the King's Club, an indoor team competition open to the best male players in Europe. Mr G wasn't short on bling either, because, in real life, he just happened to be King Gustav V of Sweden.

The king used the pseudonym to enter various tennis tournaments, perhaps forgetting that his lack of a first and second name would make him more conspicuous, not less. His enormous white moustache may also have been a giveaway, but perhaps not as much as his habit of picking the best players as his partners – including the leggy and athletic Suzanne Lenglen.

All together now – Bo!

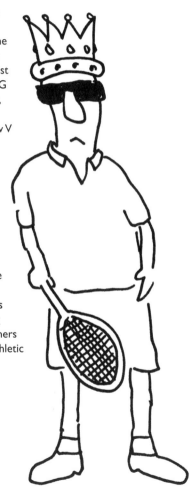

23 Hitler rants, Budge rallies
Fear on the tennis court and loathing in the *lebensraum*

If there's one person you don't want giving you a motivational talk shortly before a big game, it's Hitler. Ideal as he was for working large crowds by shrieking at them in a shrill nasal howl, it's hard to see how his unique talents would have translated to the dressing room. But that's precisely what Baron Gottfried von Cramm had to experience before his Davis Cup singles game in 1937.

Hitler called just as von Cramm was leaving the dressing room to face his American rival Don Budge. It's not known what was said – advice about topspin lobs mingled with some stuff about blood and honour, maybe – but Budge would later

remember that von Cramm had played as though his life depended on it, much as you'd expect from someone who had recently had a chat with a genocidal maniac with a hair-trigger temper.

The game turned out to be one of the greatest and most inspiring in the history of the Davis Cup. With the Führer's words ringing in his ears, von Cramm took the first two sets, only for Budge to stage an epic fightback to take the contest to a fifth set. 4–1 down, Budge rallied again and finally won 8–6.

As good a loser as he was a player, von Cramm met Budge at the net with the words "Don, this was absolutely the finest match I have ever played in my life. I'm very happy I could have played it against you, whom I like so much."

Briefly imprisoned for refusing to help promote the Nazi cause and then sent to fight on the Russian front, von Cramm managed to survive the war, but Hitler, his sports psychology business in tatters, shot himself several years later after suffering a substantial home defeat.

Bounding Basque betrayed

Tennis star wanders off course through a political minefield

Not many Wimbledon champions can boast that they've been arrested by the Nazis, arrested by the Allies and later gone on to present a trophy at the All England Club, but it was all in a day's work for Jean Borotra.

Known as "the Bounding Basque" for his habit of leaping into the crowd to kiss attractive lady spectators, Borotra blundered into controversy by agreeing to become minister of sport in the Nazi-backed republic set up in occupied France after the German invasion. He was later imprisoned by the German authorities for expressing anti-Nazi sentiments, but it didn't save him from being arrested after France was liberated in 1945 and charged with collaboration. His reputation recovered after the war, and Borotra was on hand to present Becker with his Wimbledon trophy in 1986. Nobody, happily, mentioned the war.

Teutonic travails
Hitler's bombs rain down on unfriendly Centre Court

Clearly annoyed that Gottfried von Cramm had lost three successive Wimbledon singles finals during the 1930s, the Germans used the feeble pretext of being at war to exact revenge by bombing Centre Court in October 1940 and destroying 1,200 seats. It sent a clear message to British tennis, a message which said, "You can beat our players, but nobody will be able to watch. So there."

Undaunted by this petulant display, the All England Club stayed open for the rest of the war, and was used as a base for the emergency services as well as playing host to a small farm. Repaired after the war, Centre Court was ready for play again by 1946, and to date, has proved much more durable than the thousand-year Reich.

Yvon Petra takes giant strides

The inside story of tennis's most generous inside leg

It's often said of boastful people that they are all mouth and no trousers, the implication being that they are unable to deliver on their lavish promises of high achievement. Yvon Petra was not only Wimbledon champion in the first post-war Championships, but also the owner of a pair of trousers so magnificently vast that even MC Hammer would be reduced to tears of envious rage.

The Frenchman's voluminous trouserings occupy their own place in history as the last to be worn by a Wimbledon champion – from 1947 onwards, every single men's champion has worn shorts. But as Petra was a towering six foot five, it's possible that the trousers were covering up a pair of stilts.

Either way, until fashion goes full circle and tennis trousers come back in vogue, Petra's pair remain, in every sense, the highest achieving trousers in tennis.

SECOND SET

The panties that rocked the world

A little bit of lace makes Wimbledon spin round

Britain has always had a complex relationship with sex, and its paradoxes have never been better demonstrated than by the Affair of Gussie's Panties. The Gussie in question was one Miss Gussie Moran, and her crime was to play in the 1949 Wimbledon Championships wearing lacy panties under an unusually short white tennis dress.

Amid fears that Gussie's filmy gusset might prove unequal to the job, outraged photographers and outraged spectators flocked to the court to see for themselves while outraged papers covered the outrageous panties on page after outrageous page.

One magazine summed it up best with a cover bearing the headline "Oh, Gussie!", along with a full-colour picture of the woman herself baring every inch of the offending garment with a look so knowing that it would have stopped the clock on Centre Court.

Give my regards to Broadway

Boys and show tunes see Big Bill dance down the road to perdition

Like Icarus, but with a booming forehand, Bill Tilden's death in 1953 completed the most spectacular fall from grace in the history of tennis. Known in his pomp as "Big Bill" Tilden, and possessed of the physique and power of Andy Roddick combined with the technique of Roger Federer, the muscular American dominated pre-war tennis.

He used to begin his service game with five balls in his hand – four would be served as aces and the fifth he'd cast aside with haughty disdain and the game already won. He found winning Wimbledon so easy that he simply stopped turning up in order to avoid the long sea crossing.

Unfortunately for Tilden, his fondness for choosing attractive teenage ball-boys as travelling companions cost him his reputation, his habit of squandering money on doomed Broadway shows cost him his fortune, and he died on the eve of a tournament with just over 80 dollars to his name.

Plucky Drobny wins through in the end

Try, try and try again. And again, and again and again...

Like Wimbledon's very own version of Lassie, albeit without a wet nose or a theme tune, Jaroslav Drobny overcame adversity to win through in the end, although admittedly Lassie never won Wimbledon and Drobny's trials went some way beyond forest fires or people called Jeff inexplicably falling down wells.

Born in Czechoslovakia in 1921, Drobny survived first the Nazi occupation and then Communist rule before defecting in 1949. He was reaching the end of a long career in 1954 when he finally reached the Wimbledon final at the 11th attempt, winning a thrilling final against Ken Rosewall. Even his canine counterpart would have deemed it worthy of a lie-down with a Bonio.

Rosewall holds firm

Evergreen gentleman and player enjoys a late flowering

In 1956, Ken Rosewall turned pro. As this was back in the days when amateurs were gentlemen and being paid to play was seen as the acme of vulgarity, going pro was the only way to make money on the circuit, but what made Rosewall's career remarkable was that he was still going nearly two decades later, well after the Open era had taken the stigma away from professional tennis.

He was back on Centre Court in 1974, 18 years after his first Wimbledon final, and played his last doubles match the following year. Pete Sampras paid him a memorably cryptic tribute with the words "My goal one day is to be in the same sentence as Rod Laver and Ken Rosewall." Er, what?

Breaking the colour barrier

Althea Gibson tweaks tennis's contrast control

For most of its early history, tennis was as white as Rhett Butler's country club in a Tipp-Ex snowstorm, which is why the appearance of Althea Gibson in the 1950 US Championships made history. With tennis effectively segregated, Gibson had had to play in black-only tournaments, but once she had appeared in the US Championships, she never looked back.

Gibson racked up a string of notable achievements, becoming the first black woman to win each of the four Grand Slam events, including the US, which she finally won seven years after her first appearance, and ended her career having won 11 major titles in singles and doubles.

Just as importantly, she showed the way for a host of other talented black players, all of which has been great news for tennis, and gratifyingly bad news for the kind of people who were apt to take the phrase "tennis whites" just a little too literally.

The Federation Cup starts

Sisters do it for themselves and start their own competition

The Federation Cup or "Fed Cup", as it's now abbreviated in the mistaken belief that it somehow sounds more hip, is the ladies' equivalent of the Davis Cup.

First held in 1963 and contested annually ever since, the competition is made up of regional qualifiers and two "World Groups" made up of the best teams. It may not be too surprising to hear that the USA have the best record – but the identity of its most seasoned competitor is.

Britain's very own Virginia Wade played every year between 1967 and 1983, a record of 56 singles and 44 doubles. We say "Well done, Ginny" – but could you get them to change the name to something that doesn't sound like a hiccup?

Viva Manuel Santana

Spain's greatest goes for glory in hail of upholstery

Dictators are drawn to sport like over-medalled moths to a very bright flame and Generalissimo Francisco Franco, dictator of Spain, was no exception. When Spanish tennis player Manuel Santana helped Spain to victory over the decadent imperialist running dog lackey, aka the USA, in 1965, Franco spotted the chance for a major propaganda coup.

Santana had already won the French Championships twice, and in 1966 he rewarded Spain's adoration by winning Wimbledon, although it was in the Davis Cup that he played some of his best tennis.

After the doubles win that claimed the cup for Spain, the crowd saluted Santana and partner Luis Arilla in the same way that they would hail a great matador, and pelted them with seat cushions. Being naturally more restrained, Franco settled for conventional celebrations and gave Santana a medal instead.

Steelie Jim thwarts woodworm

All change in the racket bag as metallurgy transforms tennis

Woodworm woke up to the future in 1967, and it wasn't pretty. Ever since the game of tennis had been invented, rackets had been made of their staple diet and, although racket technology had steadily improved over the years, wood was still the material of choice.

And then legendary French player René Lacoste took his design for a steel racket to Wilson. Introduced to the world as the Wilson T2000, and known as the "steelie", it became the first widely used metal racket and was soon adopted by Jimmy Connors, who won Wimbledon with it in 1982.

Today, the steelie looks like a crude relic, but the power generated by its lightweight frame helped revolutionize the game. It's now been nearly 20 years since wooden rackets were last seen at Wimbledon, and for a woodworm that's a very long time between meals.

35 Open season

Armed with accountants, players declare war on the establishment

In 1968 students took to the streets across Europe as makers of berets and Che Guevara posters worked overtime to meet the demand. Revolution was in the air and some of its unkempt fervour spilled on to the tennis court, as players realized that All you need is love was a good song, but a bad business strategy.

Playing for the love of the game would only get you so far. The big tournaments were attracting more money, but they were strictly amateur-only, so the players saw none of it. By 1968 it was decided to open competition up to professionals as well as amateurs, ushering in the "Open era".

Three of the Grand Slam tournaments dropped the word "Championships" from their names and replaced it with "Open". Wimbledon kept its "Championships", but it did have to start offering prize money for the first time. Rod Laver, the first Wimbledon champion of the Open era, received a modest £2,000. In 2005, he would have won over £600,000, demonstrating that it isn't just tournaments that are open, but also the organizers' wallets.

The marathon men

Is playing without a tie-break safe? Yes, of course it's safe...

Late one June afternoon in 1972, Pancho Gonzales and Charlie Pasarell walked out on to Centre Court at Wimbledon to play their first-round singles game. Two days and 112 games later, they finished.

As this was back in the days before the tie-break, sets had to be won by two clear games, and with neither Gonzales nor Pasarell in the mood to yield, the first ended 22–24. At 1–6 the second set was something of an anti-climax but, when play resumed the following day, the third set ballooned to an unwieldy 16–14, the fourth to a more conventional 6–3 and the fifth ended 11–9, with Gonzales the winner after surviving seven match points.

Gonzales was 41 and, with a 112-game epic behind him, it's a minor miracle that he made it as far as the fourth round before being knocked out. The tie-break was introduced to Wimbledon in 1971, ending the possibility of a repeat performance. So at five hours and 12 minutes, any players seeking to beat that record would either have to be very slow – or very, very bad.

Laver's double slam

Rocket from the Antipodes makes a second trip into the stratosphere

There's nothing like tempting fate to make you look completely stupid, which is why the Australian Davis Cup captain Harry Hopman who gave team-mate Rod Laver the ironic nickname "Rocket" must soon have regretted it.

Laver might not have been dynamic, but he had a work ethic that would have put Victorian London to shame, and in 1969 he proved it beyond doubt by becoming the first and only person to win all four Grand Slam singles titles in a year. Twice. He completed his first Grand Slam as an amateur in 1962, and the year after tennis went Open, he did it again as a professional. It might be hard to sum up Laver's legacy, but it'd be impossible to do any worse than Jim "Master of the Obvious" Courier's reflection that "You'd have to think that if he'd been around today, Rod Laver would have been Rod Laver."

CENTRE COURT

Chrissie stages an upset
Golden girl outshines the courtly star of women's tennis

Imagine, for a moment, that you're Margaret Court. It's 1970, you've staked a place in the pantheon of tennis greats by completing a Grand Slam, you're ranked number one in the world and your opponents fall before you. Then you enter an obscure tournament and lose in straight sets to a 15-year-old.

That, as they say, has got to hurt, but the 15-year-old's name was Chris Evert, and the rest is history. Evert won 18 Grand Slam singles titles, developed a memorable rivalry with Martina Navratilova and was once engaged to Jimmy Connors.

Perhaps that's why, when Evert found herself mentoring a teenage Martina Hingis, the one thing the worldly teenage prodigy asked her was not how to beat much older players – but "How do you handle men?"

One out, almost all out

Wimbledon players work to rule, but Brit vaults the barricades

Three-day weeks. Random power cuts. Work to rule. Industrial unrest and the 1970s went together like breakdowns and the Austin Allegro. Nobody was safe and, in 1973, union militancy even reached the All England Club. Or, more accurately,

the ATP – the Association of Tennis Professionals.

Yugoslavian player Nikki Pilic was denied entry to Wimbledon by his country's tennis association, which had suspended him for allegedly refusing to play in the Davis Cup. The

ATP flexed its bronzed biceps and organized a boycott, with 79 players taking part. A few big names turned up anyway, and the show went on.

The strike proved to be good news for Britain's Roger Taylor, who spotted an opening and managed to reach the semi-finals, where the plucky strikebreaker lost to eventual winner Jan Kodes. Looking back, it may have been a ploy by the trades union movement to get a British winner. And, dammit, it nearly worked.

The battle of the sexes

Chauvinistic moves held in check as King crowns herself queen

Some burned bras and others took to the streets in protest, but the battle of the sexes took on a more elegant form in September 1973 when legend of the women's game Billie Jean King played self-styled male chauvinist pig Bobby Riggs at the Houston Astrodome in one of the most famous and unorthodox games in tennis history.

Riggs was a former Wimbledon and US Open champion as well as a shameless hustler who had maintained his earning power late into his career by betting on himself in a series of one-off

challenge games, and was 55 when he achieved lasting notoriety by boasting that he could still beat any of the best female players.

To prove it, he defeated former Grand Slam winner Margaret Court in straight sets, telling the press after the game that his next feat would be to take on Billie Jean King, one of the stars of the women's game and its most vocal campaigner.

King's friend and fellow player Rosie Casals described Riggs as "an idiot", but King accepted the challenge and the "Battle of the Sexes" took place four months

later, with 30,000 tickets sold and an estimated 50 million TV viewers tuning in.

Working hard to live up to his billing as the enemy of the women's movement, Riggs, already known for wearing a t-shirt which read "Men's Liberation", came on to the court in a chariot pulled by toga-wearing models. King, not to be outdone, was brought in on a litter carried by half-naked American footballers.

For all his bragging, Riggs was still an artful and stylish player, but he was no match for the more youthful King, who won in straight sets. As gallant after the game as he had been boastful before it, Riggs said that "She was too good, too fast", but maybe his tongue had always been firmly in his cheek.

The game gave women's tennis more publicity than ever before, and after Riggs died in 1995, King described him as "a true friend for the last 25 years" and even Rosie Casals said that "he did the most for women's tennis". Now, any takers for Federer vs. Williams?

Tennis's cheekiest player

Sunlit mooning eclipses Athena's expectations

Demonstrating the truth of the maxim that nobody ever went broke by underestimating the libido of the adolescent male, high street poster shop Athena sent its profits into the stratosphere in 1977 with a poster of a young female tennis player scratching her bum.

As ubiquitous during the 1970s as crimplene, wicker and fondue, the poster's selling point was that the player, bathed in Kodachrome sunlight, was viewed from behind and by absent-mindedly raising her vestigial tennis dress in search of the itch, she was revealing bare, peachy buttocks to the camera.

This appeal to voyeurism thinly disguised as art proved hard to resist, and it's estimated that as many as two million copies of the poster have been sold to any teenage tennis fans with enough barefaced cheek to go and ask for one.

It is 1975 and you are 18. Back home in Czechoslovakia, everything is brown and people have to queue for four hours just to buy a potato, but you're in New York, playing in the US Open. Potatoes and all manner of other root vegetables are freely available here and you don't want to go home. What do you do?

This is the dilemma that Martina Navratilova faced, and, halfway through the tournament, she went to see the American authorities and arranged to defect. These authorities made young Martina feel right at home by questioning her for three hours and locking her in a hotel room with the FBI, but weeks later, the tennis world's most high-profile dissident was given her Green Card.

It proved to be a wise choice. Freed from an all-potato diet, Navratilova went on to claim more singles titles than anyone else in the Open era – including a record-breaking nine at Wimbledon alone – which just goes to show that even an Iron Curtain can't stop a woman on a mission.

King of the disco

Elton says it with song, Billie Jean says it with man-made fibres

She may have won 12 Grand Slam titles and been the most vociferous campaigner for the women's game, but a more unorthodox and less well-known part of Billie Jean King's legacy is that she provided the inspiration for Elton John's 1975 disco classic, "Philadelphia Freedom".

King and Elton had been friends for a while, and King had presented Elton with his own customized tracksuit, to which Elton responded by writing King a song. First played to her on a portable cassette player in the dressing room before a tournament, "Philadelphia Freedom" stormed up the charts.

Copies of the single – dedicated to "BJK" – are collectors' items, but history doesn't record what happened to the tracksuit.

Evonne goes walkabout
The gift to headline writers has the last laugh

In 1976, Australian tennis star Evonne Goolagong lost what would prove to be the last of four successive US Open finals. Her speed, agility and quick reflexes helped her to win the French Open, Wimbledon and the Australian Open, but never the US title; she would have won it, and maybe a Grand Slam as well, had it not been for her habit of "going walkabout".

Goolagong had a tendency to let her concentration wander at decisive moments in the game – a habit dubbed by the Australian press as "Evonne goes walkabout". As an Aborigine, Goolagong later felt that this expression was racist, as it had originally referred to Aborigines' supposed habit of wandering into the bush, but with $1.3 million in the bank by the time she retired, the joke was definitely on her critics.

Mixed singles

Sex-swap player taken to court for gender agenda

An unusual new dimension was introduced to tennis in 1975 when former Wimbledon and US Open competitor Richard Raskind had sex reassignment surgery and rejoined the tennis circuit – as Renée Richards.

When Richards's previous identity was revealed by a reporter, there was an uproar that ended in her being barred from competing in women's events. The ban was challenged in the New York Supreme Court, and Richards went on to make history by competing in the women's singles at the 1977 US Open, 17 years after making her debut in the men's.

Not everything had changed. Back in 1960, Raskind had gone out in the first round, and in 1977 Richards obligingly allayed women players' fears that her physique would give her an unfair advantage by doing exactly the same.

46 The thinking man's hostess

Superstar past of *A Question of Sport*'s mistress of the flirty aside

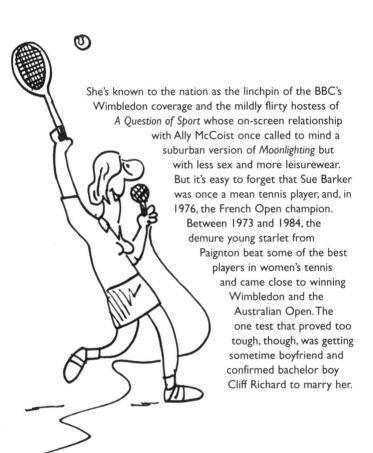

She's known to the nation as the linchpin of the BBC's Wimbledon coverage and the mildly flirty hostess of *A Question of Sport* whose on-screen relationship with Ally McCoist once called to mind a suburban version of *Moonlighting* but with less sex and more leisurewear. But it's easy to forget that Sue Barker was once a mean tennis player, and, in 1976, the French Open champion. Between 1973 and 1984, the demure young starlet from Paignton beat some of the best players in women's tennis and came close to winning Wimbledon and the Australian Open. The one test that proved too tough, though, was getting sometime boyfriend and confirmed bachelor boy Cliff Richard to marry her.

The John and George show

A beer in the hand is safer than several in the Bush

It's a well-known, if not entirely reassuring, fact that back in the days before he was just your average, simple-minded chap in charge of a large superpower, George W. Bush had something of a drink problem. Then, as now, he was prone to acting on random impulses and doing stupid things – including, back in 1976, getting arrested for drink-driving.

The officer who stopped George Junior was one Calvin Bridges, who had spotted his car weaving down the road and fined him $150. Presumably he was also given a fairly stiff parental telling-off, although given that Bush Senior became Director of the CIA the same year, he's perhaps lucky that he didn't end his days with a one-way helicopter flight over the Pacific.

Young Bush was working for President Gerald Ford's re-election campaign at the time and had attempted to drive home after having a relaxing beer (or 12) but his arrest only became known when he was running for the presidency himself over 20 years later. More of a surprise was the identity of Bush's drinking companion – Aussie tennis star John Newcombe.

Newcombe, a former world number one who had won what proved to be the last of seven Grand Slam singles titles the year before, was asked about the incident many years later in an interview on Australian network ABC TV. He had a refreshingly straightforward explanation as to what had happened. "He was 30, I was 32 and he was pretty sure he could keep up with an Australian."

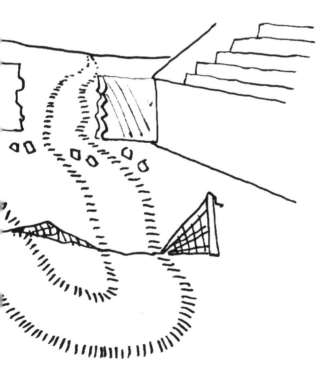

48 Victory for Ginny

Affability in the UK as Virginia wades into the competition

Despite the Sex Pistols' attempts to mar the Silver Jubilee year with artless gibberings which strangely omitted to explain what was so anarchic about selling a record to make money, Virginia Wade got things back on track in a much more congenial way by doing the decent thing and winning Wimbledon.

Wade's victory was no fluke – she had already won singles and doubles titles at the US and Australian Open and a doubles title at the French Open before her historic three-set victory over Bettie Stove in the Wimbledon ladies' singles final.

As well as being Jubilee year, 1977 was also Wimbledon's centenary year, and Her Majesty the Queen was making a rare appearance, which added to the patriotic lustre. In a rare moment of levity, the Centre Court crowd serenaded Wade by singing "For She's a Jolly Good Fellow", which made a much more pleasing sound than the Sex Pistols ever did.

Are you in there, Mr Tanner?

Cubicle crimes of a finalist used to doing time

When the American network NBC asked Wimbledon to delay the start of the 1979 men's singles final between Roscoe Tanner and Bjorn Borg by five minutes so that it could run its build-up coverage as well as some lucrative adverts, the answer, unsurprisingly, was "no". Tanner's agent – also a TV commentator – persuaded him to gain NBC the extra time by lurking longer in the lavatory. In the event, they needn't have worried.

Tanner gave them all the time they needed by taking his opponent, Bjorn Borg, to five sets before losing 6–4 in the fifth. Twenty years later, Tanner found himself buying time in a more literal fashion. Convicted of passing a bad cheque and then arrested for defaulting on child support payments, he was sent down early in 2006 for violating his probation.

When he arrived at Wimbledon in 1977, Ilie Nastase was mobbed by legions of adoring female admirers. His reception may have had less to do with his looks – short, squat and with lank black hair, he looked more like a villain from a Children's Film Foundation film than a ladykiller – than his bad boy reputation.

Nastase's antics on court were the stuff of legend. He got down on his hands and knees to inspect the Cyclops machine and borrowed an umbrella from a spectator while receiving serve. But the mercurial Romanian could also go from jovial horseplay to outright anger in a heartbeat, as some players – and at least one spectator – found out to their cost.

When he became aware that someone in the crowd had been zealously clapping all his mistakes, Nastase turned to her and delivered the immortal line, "If you don't shut up, I'm going to shit in your hat."

Three's a crowd

Foetal misunderstanding costs Margaret court time

Singles involves having two people on the court at a time, and doubles involves four. Margaret Court, arguably one of the greatest tennis players of all time, brought a glittering career to an end when she realized that there were three.

Court had reached the quarter-final of a singles tournament in 1977 – and defaulted after discovering that she was pregnant. Her other claim to fame was that she had won a "boxed set" of Grand Slam titles, by winning singles, ladies' doubles and mixed doubles at all four of the Grand Slam events. To date, though, she seems to be the first player to have played "triples"…

52 Flushing Meadows

There's a bright golden haze on the tennis court

Easily the most pastoral-sounding venue in tennis, Flushing Meadows Park evokes lyrical visions of acres of rolling grassland, cows lazily chewing the cud and swallows scudding overhead. The reality is that it's in the heart of Queens in New York City – and, since 1978, home to the US Open.

Originally the venue for the 1939–40 World's Fair, Flushing Meadows was the first home – albeit briefly – of the United Nations and is now home to the USTA National Tennis Center. The centre court is known as Arthur Ashe Stadium, after the famous former champion, but the reasoning behind the name of the second court is more of a mystery – it's the Louis Armstrong Stadium.

Taking umpirage

Hapless Hammond fails to measure up to mob rule

Tennis is a spectator sport, and genteel rounds of applause and the occasional shout of "Come on, Tim" by the naïve and over-enthusiastic are part of the auditory clutter of Wimbledon. Sadly, they do things differently overseas, and seldom have the crowd had a more direct influence on the game than in Ilie Nastase's meeting with John McEnroe in the 1979 US Open.

Nastase was in one of his livelier moods, and umpire Frank Hammond, deciding that things had gone far enough, defaulted him. The crowd, presumably made up of the kind of New Yorkers who would deem a lukewarm coffee to be a fatal insult, promptly rioted.

Among a hail of beer cans, tournament director Mike Blanchard reinstated Nastase before dismissing the umpire and taking his place. McEnroe won, and decorum went limping from the tournament, never to be seen again.

I spy with an electric eye

All-seeing Cyclops becomes a blinking nuisance

Ah, the Wimbledon highlights package. Generally made up of footage of people amusing themselves during rain delays, attractive girls from the Home Counties looking demure and slow-motion replays of a British hopeful losing and/or falling over, they're not complete without one player getting down on his hands and knees and glaring at a small box beside the service line.

The box contains the device known as Cyclops. First installed at the All England Club way back in

1980, Cyclops was designed by Bill Carlton, a former aircraft engineer. It helps the line judges make more accurate line calls by sending an infra-red beam past the service line. When a ball breaks the beam, Cyclops beeps to warn of a foul service. Or at least that's the theory.

Cyclops is formidably accurate and has helped remove the random element introduced to umpiring by sleepy line judges who have to spend hour after hour concentrating beneath the blazing sun with nothing to protect their

sanity save a straw hat – but for all that, it can still go wrong.

Random bleeps have been produced by a pigeon taking a casual saunter along the side of the court during a game, an errant insect or simply because Cyclops sometimes likes to clear its throat at a particularly fraught moment.

When Tim Henman played Dmitry Tursunov in the second round in 2005, both felt that Cyclops was not working and asked for it to be turned off. The umpire merely shrugged, causing even the perennially nice Tim to come back with the sarcastic reply, "That's the reaction I love to see. That fills us with confidence."

Experiments with fully automated systems at the US and Australian Open, which even offer action replays, suggest that Cyclops' days could be numbered, but that would deprive highlights package compilers of that other great stand-by: the good, old-fashioned line-call-related strop. What do you say to that, Cyclops?

"Beep."

55 Iceborg vs. The Brat

Bjorn keeps his cool as petulant pretender wilts

Ladies and gentlemen! In the ice-blue corner we present Bjorn Borg, winner of four Wimbledon titles and a defending champion possessed of such glacial cool that we know him as "Iceborg". In the very, very red corner, we present the challenger, John McEnroe, owner of a temper so volcanic that it could power most of Surrey, baiter of umpires and a precocious new tennis talent.

Such was the line-up for the 1980 men's singles final, which is perhaps one of the greatest games of tennis ever played. In this marathon five-setter, Borg had a total of seven match points in the fourth, but McEnroe saved them all and took the set 18–16 on a tie-break.

Borg, implacable as ever, shrugged off a psychological setback that would have felled a lesser man, and took the fifth, 8–6. Recalling the game many years later, he said, with characteristic understatement, "the tennis was good that day".

"You Cannot be Serious"

Wilde at heart McEnroe becomes king of the angry epigram

McEnroe had a temper to match his explosive tennis, and both were on display at Wimbledon in 1981. Playing against Tim Gullikson, McEnroe believed he had seen chalk dust kicked up by his serve, indicating that it was in. He approached the umpire's chair, and a ripple of excitement ran around the crowd. This was what they had paid to see. Superbrat vs. Umpire, the smackdown. Live.

They weren't disappointed. McEnroe bellowed out, "You cannot be serious," with just the right whining nasal inflection at the end to invoke images of a petulant teenager, adding "you guys are the pits of the earth". The umpire, Edward James, deducted a point from McEnroe, who then called him an incompetent fool.

McEnroe went on to win the singles title that year, but he still had enough bile left to conjure up one final wrathful retort. He refused to attend the winners' dinner, he said, because he didn't want to sit with "a bunch of stiffs who were 70–80 years old, telling you that you're acting like a jerk". Ouch.

57 Buster, Buster give us a song

Don't be stupid, be a smarty, come and join Mottram's party

British tennis players are used to making the short journey from hero to pariah, but Buster Mottram managed it in emphatic fashion. In 1983, plucky old Buster peaked at number 15 in the rankings, making him the last British player before Henman to break into the top 20. So far, so good.

And then, when his career ended, Buster decided to go into politics. The problem was that Buster's chosen party was the National Front, which alienated many of his former fans. Buster then alienated the National Front by striking up a songwriting partnership with black comedian Kenny Lynch.

With nobody left to alienate, he returned to obscurity, leaving a gap in the extreme right-wing tennis songwriting market that, strangely, has never been filled.

58 Lendl turns up the power

Ivan the powerful carries all before him

Spectators might not have guessed that they were watching the end of one era and the beginning of another, but that's exactly what Ivan Lendl's defeat of John McEnroe in the 1984 French Open final represented.

Despite being two sets down, Lendl staged a muscular comeback, bludgeoning McEnroe out of the game with what became known as "power tennis". With his booming serve, powerful forehand and zealous attention to his fitness, Lendl proved to be the first of a new breed.

This approach won Lendl eight Grand Slam titles, but the time in the gym did cost him in other ways. Although Lendl was the first player to turn the power up to 11, the charisma control stayed firmly in the minus numbers. He wasn't quite the Steve Davis of tennis, but he was as close as you could get without a polyester waistcoat.

59 Boris Becker booms in

Big-serving German hits a purple patch

One of the entrants to Wimbledon in 1985 was an unknown and unseeded German teenager. With names like McEnroe and Lendl in the draw, his progress went unnoticed. He faced match point in the second round and an injured ankle in the third, but even before he beat Anders Jarryd to reach the final, pundits had realized that Boris Becker was going to be a name to remember.

Becker's booming serve blew Kevin Curren out of the final, and carried the German into the history books as the first unseeded Wimbledon champion and, at 17, the tournament's youngest men's singles champion.

The All England broke out the German flags, while Becker proved that, despite being the Wimbledon champion, he was still a German teenager at heart. Heading dutifully back to his room, Boris rocked out to the sounds of his favourite band – geriatric metal merchants Deep Purple.

Vintage Connors just too strong

Jimmy uncorks a classic performance to claim the winner's bouquet

Anyone who remembers the 1970s weepie *The Champ* may recall how Jon Voight, a boxer past his prime, risked all in the ring for one last payday. Similar thoughts came to mind when 34-year-old former Wimbledon champion Jimmy Connors made what seemed like a similarly doomed bid to roll back the years in his clash with Mikael Pernfors.

Connors was trailing Pernfors 6–1, 6–1, 4–1 and carrying a leg injury. It seemed that all the game lacked was a tearful child sobbing, "Wake up, daddy." But, unlike Voight's character, Connors refused to lie down and die, and brawled his way back to win the game 6–2 in the fifth.

It was one of Wimbledon's greatest-ever comebacks, and taught the world that you don't always have to be beaten to death to treat the punters to a pathos-laden sports classic.

Emotions. Different players deal with them in different ways. McEnroe
vented them on the umpires, while Tim Henman's clenched fist is so
at odds with the rest of his personality that it makes him look like a
Mondeo driver who has just found the last parking space at the retail
park. But you'd have to go a long way to beat Pat Cash's performance at
Wimbledon in 1987.

It was the year after *Crocodile Dundee* and *Neighbours* had reached
Britain, and Australia was more ubiquitous than at any time since Rolf
Harris had first put his name to the Stylophone. Cash might not have been
the top seed, he might have worn a black-and-white headband that made
him look like one of the kids from *Fame*, but this wave of empathy with
the Antipodes carried him into the final.

His opponent was Ivan Lendl. The Czech player was the world number
one, but had lost to Becker in the previous year and the only thing he
would ever win at the All England was the unwelcome label "defeated

finalist". Cash won in straight sets, surviving a tie-break in the first and ending on 7–6, 6–2, 7–5.

It was what happened next that made history. Instead of making awkward small talk with his vanquished opponent, Cash leapt into the crowd, making for his family and friends who were seated several rows up in the visitors' box.

In a few short bounds, Cash turned a mundane final into a memorable one, and created a form of celebration that has been seen many times since. Suddenly, having a bit of a weep didn't seem to come close to conveying the kind of emotion that you were supposed to feel after winning a Championship.

Cash should have copyrighted it, because that year's Wimbledon proved to be the zenith of a career that was later disrupted by injury. Britain faced an equally bleak future. Despite the old country having embraced Cash as one of its own, the response from Australia was savage. *Home and Away* aired the following year.

Bagels and humble pie

Bread with the hole in the middle sums up the emptiness of defeat

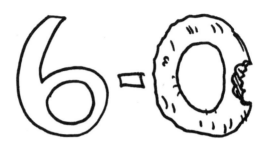

Wining a set 6–0 is known as a bagel after the similarity of the dread zero to the doughy snack. Manage this feat in consecutive games, and you've got yourself a double bagel which, in three-set events, is enough to send your opponent back to the changing room having failed to win a single game.

Steffi Graf double-bageled Natasha Zvereva at the French Open final in 1988 and Lleyton Hewitt double-bageled Alex Corretja at the Australian Open in 2000, but the prize for serving up the greatest bagel of all time goes to Stefan Edberg.

In what was arguably the tennis equivalent of a deluxe bagel with cream cheese, salmon and a host of other savoury delights, the implacable Edberg added a new delicacy called "pulverized Swede" to the traditional mix by completing a rare triple bagel against hapless countryman Stefan Eriksson at Wimbledon in 1987.

Melbourne Park

Patriotic calls for bloodshed at a park Down Under

When the new venue for the Australian Open was completed in 1988, the local tennis establishment decided to give it the staggeringly imaginative name "Melbourne Park", thereby preventing any misunderstandings. They might have done better to call it Mark Edmondson Park instead.

The embarrassing fact is that Edmondson was the last Australian to win the men's singles at the Open and that was way back in 1976. Since then, many have tried, and all have failed, including seven Aussie winners of other Grand Slam titles. Pat Cash came heartbreakingly close, going to five sets in 1987 and 1988, but even the hyper-confident Hewitt choked in the final in 2005.

Disgusted John Newcombe has said that in his day, "as an Australian you never left the court losing unless you had blood all over you". He may have a point, but calling it the Bloodbath Arena may be one name change too far.

Graf's Olympic dream

Steffi's golden glow outshines Austin's minor achievements

After beating a 13-year-old German teenager in 1982, Tracy Austin dismissed her defeated opponent with the words: "There are hundreds of players like her in America." Six years later, Steffi Graf became the first and, to date only, person to win a Golden Slam.

Graf won a conventional Slam in 1988, which just so happened to be the first year since 1924 that tennis had been included at the Olympics, although it had been one of the events at the first of the modern games in 1896. She wasted no time seizing the opportunity, and duly won gold in Seoul later that year, completing a unique Golden Slam.

Tracy Austin's reaction – like the location of the "hundreds" of American players capable of a similar achievement – remains unknown.

THIRD SET

Every day isn't like Sunday

Silent and grey days force Wimbledon to rethink its timetable

Desperate circumstances call for desperate measures, even for bastions of tradition like the All England Club. Facing a fixtures backlog in 1991 when play was disrupted by that other great British tradition – the midsummer torrential downpour – it took an unprecedented step and held play on the middle Sunday.

Calling it "People's Sunday" – as though the Club had suddenly been taken over by a Marxist-Leninist collective and a red flag flew above its green acres – may have been inaccurate, but an egalitarian impulse was in the air. All tickets, even those for Centre Court, would be allocated on a first-come, first-served basis.

Demonstrating that some traditions will always endure, fans quickly got on with the serious business of forming an orderly queue. It was such a success that it was repeated again in 1997 and 2004, but the future of People's Sunday has been threatened by a bourgeois new development. Centre Court is due to get a roof.

"Ooh, I say..."

Classic of understatement from the master of moderation

Like a knowledgeable granddad whose mellifluous tone was redolent of a bygone age when reserve ruled, Dan Maskell was the voice of tennis for legions of Wimbledon watchers, and his trademark exclamation is legendary.

Nobody knows when he first said, "Ooh, I say", but it seemed to sum up the Championships' urbane, understated charm. Superb cross-court backhand? An awed and approving "Ooh, I say". Petulant player having a tantrum?

A disapproving "Ooh, I say". Three words, suitable for a wide range of situations.

Maskell last uttered them on air in 1991, retiring that year after his 40th Wimbledon, and, sadly, died the following year, but his contribution to the tournament is not likely to be forgotten.

Whenever someone hits a passing shot from an impossible angle, you too can have some of that Maskell magic in your very own living room – simply repeat... "Ooh, I say..."

The iceborg melts

Steep comeback trail leaves glacial Swede hot and bothered

You can forgive your idols many things. Lapses of judgement, eclipse by younger players, even launching their own brand of underwear, but it's hard to smile on the comeback bid which makes a travesty of all that they once were, and few comebacks were more ill-advised than Bjorn Borg's in 1991.

Borg had retired in 1983, and to anyone for whom Borg meant Kodachrome-tinted 70s summers and whose Fila-branded sportswear was the acme of cool, watching him making an unsuccessful return to a sport that he had dominated eight years before was like finding Elvis playing the pub circuit.

He was beaten on a regular basis by the kind of players that he'd once have pounded into the ground, and as if the results weren't bad enough, Borg added an extra layer of doomed nostalgia by using a wooden racket. He eventually gave up in favour of the seniors' circuit, and headbands and wooden rackets went the way of loon pants and spacehoppers.

Wimbledon queue goes alfresco

As the rain pours down, the crowd breaches its banks

The Wimbledon queue took on a life of its own in 1992 with the introduction of "Middle Saturday". In a bid to re-create the atmosphere seen the previous year – when rain delays led to the creation of "People's Sunday", when anyone could queue for a ticket – the same principle was applied to what became known, with a thrilling lack of imagination, as "People's Saturday".

By 2002, people were arriving in droves on Friday night, and a most un-Wimbledon outbreak of violence over queueing etiquette meant that the ticket allocation was reduced, but the queue of tents and sleeping bags still lines the road the night before. Like bin day outside Millets.

Clown Prince Henry

Leconte proves that there's more to French comedy than mime

Henry VIII might have been the first famous Henry in tennis, but ask fans who their favourite is and they'll almost certainly nominate Henri Leconte. He never quite managed to win a Grand Slam event, but with charisma to spare and an attitude that suggested he never took the game completely seriously, Leconte was always one to watch.

Even in 1993, during a semi-final against Becker at Wimbledon, a game that represented Leconte's last shot at Grand Slam singles title glory, he responded to the pressure in his own unique way.

Others would have opted for fist-pumping aggression, but not Leconte. Instead, he killed time by bouncing the ball on his own head and pretending to shoot Boris Becker with his tennis racket. Leconte lost the game, but was later offered some lucrative engagements on the children's party circuit.

Angry spouse lashes out as husband crashes out

They say that hell hath no fury like a woman scorned, but in the wake of Benedicte Tarango's performance at Wimbledon in 1995 the hoary old truism should perhaps be revised to "hell hath no fury like a tennis wife run amok".

Mrs Tarango did not react well when husband Jeff Tarango stormed off court having accused the French umpire of being corrupt. Siding with her spouse, she soon found the official who had gone off to tell the relevant authorities, and, like a Valkyrie but with a more expensive manicure, slapped him. Minutes later she was telling all to stunned journalists and a gleeful husband at a press conference.

It could have been worse. Jeff Tarango had been in trouble the year before at a tournament in Tokyo – for mooning to the crowd.

Sir Cliff sings in the rain

Shadows fall on Centre Court as England's Elvis goes solo

He liked small speakers. He liked tall speakers. And at a very wet Wimbledon in 1996, finding himself wired for sound, Sir Cliff Richard seized the moment as only he could.

Realizing that yet another downpour was making itself comfortable for the afternoon, long-time tennis fan and Wimbledon spectator Sir Cliff reached for the microphone to help raise the spirits of the stoic few sitting it out around Centre Court beneath their umbrellas.

Tastefully attired in the uniform of the middle-aged pop aristocracy – to wit, a checked jacket and nice thin tie, Sir Cliff hit them with a medley of popular hits, including the inevitable "Singing in the Rain".

Demonstrating that Brits will happily make fools of themselves provided someone else takes the lead, the remnants of the crowd joined in, but Sir Cliff also had some unusually high-profile backing singers.

This being Wimbledon, where you could scarcely fling a strawberry without the errant fruit striking a former champion, Martina Navratilova and Pam Shriver both helped Sir Cliff out, along with Virginia Wade and Conchita Martinez.

Despite repeated requests, Sir Cliff has since refused to reprise his performance, and whether or not "Bachelor Boy" is one of your desert island discs, the one-off concert has the kind of game, laughing-in-the-face-of-adversity jollity that you could only experience at Wimbledon.

Sadly, Sir Cliff seems to think differently and has said that he feels like "hiding in the toilets" whenever it starts to rain and he finds himself in the crowd. We think you might be being a bit too hard on yourself, Sir Cliff, unless the toilets at SW19 are a good place to hear yourself. In stereo. Stereo. Stereo. Stereo.

72 Tiger Tim sees red

Ball-girl gets an earful when Heman hits a thunderbolt

A year before Henmania gripped the nation, emotion of a different sort gripped Henman himself on Wimbledon's Court 14 in 1995, when he challenged his nice guy persona too successfully by becoming the first person to be disqualified from Wimbledon. His crime? Hitting a ball down court in anger.

It might not sound like a heinous offence, but Henman had perhaps struck the ball lower and harder than he had realized, with the result that it hit ball-girl Caroline Hall. In the ear. It had been an accident, but you don't get to be the All England referee by bending the rules, and Alan Mills duly disqualified Henman.

Mortified in a way that you can't quite imagine from either McEnroe or Nastase, Henman apologized profusely and presented the ball-girl, and her throbbing ear, with flowers, thus bringing to an end a brief – and unlikely – career as the bad boy of Court 14.

73 Henmania

Virulent strain of optimism gives sufferers delusions of glory

As well as being the year that football came home, shortly before leaving for Germany, 1996 was also the year that Tim Henman became the first British player to get through to the Wimbledon quarter-finals since Roger Taylor in 1973. The achievement caught the mood of a sport-mad nation, and the ailment known as "Henmania" was born.

A strange disease that has since gripped British tennis fans every summer, it causes otherwise sensible people to wear ridiculous clothes and shout "Come on, Tim!" at tense moments, but its most marked symptom is a complete detachment from reality.

The belief that "this is Tim's year" persists through double faults, dropped service games, broken serves and needlessly fraught five-setters against obscure no-hopers. And the only cure for this strange syndrome? A trip to the local bookie to see just how long those odds really are.

The Woodies
Sturdy doubles partnership takes its final bow

If anyone ever asks you about medal-winning woodies, back away slowly. Unless, of course, they're talking about tennis. As well as having the sport's most snigger-worthy nickname, the Woodies were Mark Woodforde and Todd Woodbridge, two Australians who were the most prolific doubles partnership and who proved it once and for all in 1996 when they won Olympic gold.

Winning the Olympic title was the high point of what would eventually become a 10-year partnership. By the time Mark Woodforde decided to call it a day in 2000, they had completed a career Grand Slam of doubles titles, including six Wimbledons, two Australian Opens, two US Opens and a single French Open, as well as 12 Masters Series titles, and helped Australia to win the Davis Cup.

The two complemented each other perfectly. Known for his volleying skills, the ginger-haired Woodforde was the older of the pair and a left-hander, while Woodbridge, who had quick reflexes and superb agility, was a right-hander.

The pair won their last Wimbledon title together in 2000, but weeks afterwards lost an emotional defence of their Olympic title in front of their home crowd at the Sydney Olympics, and had to settle for silver as a consolation prize. Later that year, Woodforde retired after Australia lost the Davis Cup to Spain, but Woodbridge, scenting the whiff of burning record books, carried on.

With Jonas Bjorkman as his new partner, the lone Woodie continued his winning ways, and in January 2004 passed Tom Okker's record of 78 career doubles titles. By the time he retired in 2005, he had won a further five Grand Slam doubles since playing with Woodforde, three of them at Wimbledon, taking him past the Doherty brothers' record of eight doubles titles at the Championships.

To have one prize-winning Woodie is fortunate, but to have another which also breaks records is very fortunate indeed, and so, tennis's proudest and most prolific Woodies, we salute you.

A-pinny-onated streaker

Boring final dusted down by underdressed maid

Ask anyone if they remember much about the tennis played in the 1996 final between MaliVai Washington and Richard Krajicek, and the most likely response will be a look of blank bafflement. Ask them if they remember anything else, and the answer will be "the streaker".

Wimbledon's first-ever streaker could not have picked a more opportune final in which to make a debut. Neither Krajicek nor Washington was blessed with great talent or charisma, so if the pre-match build-up needed anything, it needed an attractive blonde in nothing but a tiny apron, and that's exactly what it got.

People were still talking about it years later. When a male streaker made an appearance at the Australian Open, commentator John Lloyd thought back fondly to the summer of '96, reflecting with some accuracy, "That was a better sight. That was a female."

Exploding blondeshell
Kournikova's powerful put-down cuts admirers down to size

Anna Kournikova might not have lived up to her early potential, with a wobbly serve and a string of injuries contributing to an early end to her career, but her looks generated more column inches than a Grand Slam winner and sold more magazines than a month of exclusives, and she had a precocious attitude to match the sex kitten image.

She came up with the all-time best put-down in women's tennis. Faced with unwelcome but unsurprising attention from a group of young male fans, the 17-year-old prodigy calmly sauntered past and remarked, "You can't afford me, boys."

Superstitious minds

Lucky Lindsay puts her hands in the air like she just doesn't care

Winning the US Open in 1998 meant that Lindsay Davenport finally got to hold a trophy over her head. The reason for this was not some debilitating arm injury, but the fact that Davenport is one of a number of superstitious tennis players.

Davenport will reportedly only hold a trophy over her head if it was won at a Grand Slam event – all others are held against her head or body. It may sound bizarre, but

compared to others on the circuit Davenport is positively normal.

Marat Safin uses an evil eye to ward off bad vibes, Jelena Dokic wears the same clothes throughout a tournament, Goran Ivanisevic used to eat the same food at the same table in the same restaurant at Wimbledon and Martina Hingis always tries to avoid stepping on white tramlines – quite a handicap for a tennis player.

Battling Agassi completes his Slam

Crowd left breathless as ecstatic Andre clears the final hurdle

No male tennis player has managed to win a Grand Slam since Rod Laver in 1969, but for old warhorses who have galloped around the circuit for a while, one objective is still within reach – the career Grand Slam. And in 1999, Andre Agassi finally completed his.

The French Open had always been Agassi's bogey tournament, but at that year's final he beat Andrei Medvedev, despite having lost the first two sets of a match that had been as emotionally draining for the crowd as it had been for the players.

He's still going, but there are signs that time has taken its toll. After losing the 2005 Australian Open final to Federer, Agassi was asked what they had talked about at the net. "He told me how much he enjoyed playing me," Agassi said, "and that he hoped it happens a lot more in the future. That makes one of us."

Bonking Boris gets cupboard love

Restaurant reprise of "Love In An Elevator" strikes the wrong note

Adding a whole new meaning to the idea of service, the youngest winner of the men's title at Wimbledon proved that he had lost none of his boyish zeal in June 1999 when he conceived a child in a restaurant cupboard with Russian model Angela Ermakova.

Telling all in an autobiography appropriately called *Stay a Moment Longer*, Boris said that he got talking to Ermakova in the restaurant and, with the blushing coyness of the true romantic, "got down to business in the most convenient place". Eight months later, Ermakova, clearly something of an old romantic herself, told Becker that he was due to be a father. By fax.

With the scandal already public knowledge, Becker and his wife divorced the following year. The name of the restaurant, by some terrible quirk of fate that must have delighted the tabloids, was Nobu. Insert your own pun here.

80 Daddy uncool

Damir Dokic: not waving, not drowning, just gesticulating madly

Poor old Jelena Dokic. Her family fled Croatia in fear of the coming civil war and ended up emigrating to Australia, but young Jelena revealed a talent for tennis that suggested a brighter future. She conquered Kim Clijsters and vanquished Venus Williams, but the one thing she couldn't overcome was her decidedly odd father.

Damir Dokic was also his daughter's coach, but for all that his advice pushed her along the path to stardom, his behaviour helped pull her back the other way. In 1999 he was ejected from a tournament in Edgbaston for calling club officials "Nazis", and then arrested after lying down in the road in protest.

Showing true dedication to the cause, he was then thrown out of Wimbledon and the US Open the following year, and accused of assaulting a cameraman at the Australian Open, but the chances of him achieving a bad-boy Grand Slam are slim: annoyed by his antics, his daughter has sacked him.

The Williams Family

Paternal pride proves too strange a brew for the outraged establishment

Their house is a museum, where people come to see 'em, they really are a scre-am, the Williams Family. Admittedly, their house isn't actually a museum, but by every other criterion in the Addams Family theme tune, the Williamses are tennis's most entertaining – and often, in the person of Richard Williams, most bizarre – family.

The story of Williams picking up syringes on the courts of Compton so that his daughters could practise has lost its shock value, but it does demonstrate his determination – as well as a tendency to write himself into the heart of the script.

Realizing how much money could be made from tennis, Williams reportedly told his wife: "We need to make two more kids". As a plea to the fleshy glories of human love it fell short of Donne or Keats but, as the result was Venus and Serena, it must have worked.

Winning Wimbledon was the embryonic players' goal, and in 2000 Venus became the first of

the pair to achieve it, but Williams Senior was also coming into his own. Giving interviews to anyone who cared to listen, he made use of those annoyingly quiet spells also known as "tennis matches" by holding up signs to the courtside TV cameras.

The most famous of these read "I need an ice-cold Coca-Cola," although he may as well have written "Please pay me attention" At the moment of Venus's victory, he danced on the roof of the commentary box, inflicting literally minutes of terror on the occupants, including Chris Evert who "thought the roof was coming down".

It would be churlish to deny Williams his triumphs, but when someone describes his daughter being booed, as "the worst act of prejudice I've seen since they killed Martin Luther King", you've got to wonder about their priorities.

Still, he did hold up another sign saying "British fans are the best in the world," which happens to be true, so we'll let him off.

The Three Gorans of the Apocalypse

Multiple personalities ride to the rescue as greatness beckons

Pages from the form book were cast to the wind in a whirlwind of emotion at Wimbledon in 2001 when the mercurial wild card entrant and world No. 125 Goran Ivanisevic beat the former US Open champion Pat Rafter in an epic three-hour, five-set final. His secret? That there are, in fact, three Gorans.

The existence of good Goran, bad Goran and emergency Goran was revealed in a characteristically unorthodox press conference after he had beaten Andy Roddick in four sets. "Bad Goran" is, apparently, sometimes known as "crazy Goran" and normally surfaces when all is lost, including his temper.

This wayward temper raised the destruction of rackets from a mere code violation to a work of performance art. He had to retire from the Samsung Open in Brighton

in 2000 having smashed all his rackets, turning to supervisor Gerry Armstrong with the words "Gerry, I have no more rackets left."

The following year, his tennis was still frustrating him, but his racket-throwing technique was perfected. "I tossed it nicely," he said once. "No warning, beautiful. That's the art of throwing rackets." So when the combative Croat was given a wild card at Wimbledon, nobody took him seriously. Until he reached the final.

The three Gorans had already lost three previous finals, one to Agassi and two to Sampras, but with good Goran keeping bad Goran in check, with the exception of a brief return to net-kicking, racket-throwing form in the fourth set, good old emergency Goran timed his appearance to perfection.

After blowing two match points on double faults and losing a third when Rafter caught him out with a lob, emergency Goran finally arrived during the 16th game of the fifth set in the shape of a blistering serve that was too powerful for Rafter. The three Gorans took the set and the Championship, 6–3, 3–6, 6–3, 2–6, 9–7.

His triumphant return to his home town, Split, suggested that there was one Goran that the world had yet to see. Overcome by the emotion of 150,000 fans, Ivanisevic stripped down to his underwear and unveiled Largely Naked Goran.

83 Melanie Molitor's apron strings

Misfiring Martina finds the ties that bind are just too strong

It's often said – normally by mothers, oddly enough – that mother knows best, but in the case of Martina Hingis and mother Melanie Molitor, it seems to be true. Named "coach of the year" in 1997, Melanie had named her daughter after Martina Navratilova and had her playing at the age of two.

Her reward was a daughter who won Wimbledon at 16 and came close to winning a Grand Slam. But two years later the relationship went into meltdown following Hingis's display of Olympic-standard petulance at the 1999 French Open final against Steffi Graf, and a tirade of abuse in which Amelie Mauresmo was described as "half man".

Molitor was sacked, albeit briefly, and Hingis finally retired at the great age of 22. Retirement didn't last long and, late in 2005, Hingis announced that she was about to make a comeback. Her coach? Melanie Molitor.

If anyone is destined to bring forth into the world a future tennis star, it's Steffi Graf. Winner of 22 Grand Slam singles titles, the only winner of the Golden Slam and a former No. I who held the top spot for a record 377 weeks, Graf is the highest-ranked player to have retired – and, since 2001, the wife of Andre Agassi.

The couple already have two children, a boy and a girl and, possibly taking his rivalry with Pete Sampras a little too far, Agassi once said that "If Pete's child is a girl, my son will like her; if he's a boy, my son will defeat him."

Still, with both the Graf and Agassi children not long out of nappies, it'll be some time before either is challenging for honours, so in the meantime we'll just have to make do with the family's other gift to the world – a seemingly infinite variety of T-Mobile adverts.

85 Serena, Venus and Bart too

Springfield's finest lose a game but gain a wallet when superstars call

Proving that even without the full complement of fingers you can still join the ranks of the tennis immortals, *The Simpsons* extended a friendly, if mis-shapen, yellow paw to the world of tennis with a star-studded themed episode.

Beginning with the Simpsons' decision to build their own tennis court, events take a typically dysfunctional turn as Marge and Homer make a more ambitious choice of partner to increase their chances of winning a tournament. Lisa is replaced by Venus Williams and Bart by Serena, only for Marge and Homer to be replaced by Pete Sampras and Andre Agassi.

The real players voice their own characters – although Agassi's lines are limited to "I'm Andre Agassi" – and the episode ends with Homer stealing Sampras's wallet and drawing the conclusion "it's better to watch stuff than do stuff".

Super 9 superlatives

Pinnacle of achievement remains unconquered, but Agassi climbs the highest

For tennis fans whose year is structured around the four Grand Slam events, the Super 9 might sound like a brand of engine oil, but this set of nine separate tournaments played in Europe and North America presents a tough challenge in its own right, and in 2002 Andre Agassi became its uncrowned king.

Nobody has ever won all nine events, either in a single year or even during the course of their careers, but when Agassi beat Tommy Haas in Rome, he added a record seventh tournament to his total. Only Monte Carlo and Hamburg still eluded him, but two contenders to his title have begun to emerge.

In 2005, Federer and Nadal both won four of the nine, with Tomas Berdych being the only other member of the tour to get a look-in, and until the Super 9 finally falls, the Fantastic Four is still no mean feat.

Caught short

Struggling stars find that time in the smallest room is seldom wasted

Depending on your point of view, the bathroom break is either a necessary part of the game or the last refuge of the player about to lose, but there's no doubt that deciding to nip back to the locker-room toilets for a relaxing five minutes alone with the paper can work wonders, as Pete Sampras demonstrated in 2002.

A noticeably weary Sampras was playing against Agassi in the singles final of the US Open and, after losing the third set, decided to take a visit to the bathroom. And then came out to win the game in the fourth.

It can be taken too far, though. Andy Roddick took longer than usual when he found himself caught short in the middle of his Australian Open match with Lleyton Hewitt, which gave the Aussie firebrand an opportunity to showcase his new man credentials. "Ten minutes?" Hewitt seethed. "That's the women. It's not for the men; not for the real game, mate."

Pistol Pete's millions

Sampras's firepower proves enough to break the bank

Tournament organizers around the world breathed a sigh of relief in 2003 when Pete Sampras zipped up his racket bag for the last time. Sampras won the Wimbledon men's singles title seven times, a record that is unlikely ever to be beaten, won seven other Grand Slam titles and 11 Masters Series finals, but it's his earnings that really set him apart from the chasing pack.

Sampras took home a record total of $43 million in prize money during his long career, over $10 million more than second-placed earner Andre Agassi who, having only banked a paltry $29.5 million, was positively skint by comparison. It proves that the man they called "Pistol Pete" didn't earn his nickname – or his millions – by holding up banks.

89 RUDE-sedski
Greg's expensive expletives upset viewers

Any game of tennis at Wimbledon involving a British player attracts a degree of partisan shouting. "Come on, Tim", "Come on, Andy" and "Come on, Greg" are all familiar refrains. The one thing you shouldn't do is shout "out." During a rally.

Greg Rusedski's game against Andy Roddick in 2003 showed why. Rusedski was 5–2 up in the third set and about to return a forehand when someone shouted "out". Assuming he'd won the point, he stopped playing, but the someone was a spectator. Denied

a chance to replay the point, Rusedski lost it. In every sense.

He embarked on an expletive-laden tirade which the BBC microphones caught and broadcast in its uncensored glory, resulting in numerous angry letters from viewers. Sadly, nobody was angrier than Greg, who went on to lose the set and, with it, the match.

John McEnroe, with the weariness of someone who has been there, and paid the fine, observed: "I was counting the thousands as the words progressed."

Wimbledon: the movie

British film-makers project their tennis dream on to the silver screen

"She's the golden girl. He's the longshot…" ran the tagline for *Wimbledon*, the tennis rom-com shot at the Championships in 2003. It might also have added "…and you know exactly what happens next", but when it comes to films about plucky Brits valiantly attempting to win Wimbledon against impossible odds, fiction could scarcely be more predictable than the more bitter reality.

The plot centres around one such Brit, washed-up pro Paul Colt, and a seemingly doomed bid to win Wimbledon. Having been made by the same people who brought you *Four Weddings* and *Notting Hill*, the film also features an equally implausible bid to woo a young American tennis starlet, who, unlike most young American tennis starlets, clearly isn't turned off by the noxious whiff of failure.

Paul duly battles through to the final and, although we won't spoil the ending, it wouldn't be giving too much away to say that it doesn't end in a downward spiral of despair, drugs and disillusion.

Not everybody was impressed when organizers of the 2004 Madrid Masters decided to use nubile female fashion models as ball-girls. Their vestigial skirts and clinging vest tops were a hit with photographers but not with Soledad Murillo. The Spanish government's secretary for equality raged that it encouraged women to be seen as objects of "decoration and entertainment".

Agassi struck a diplomatic note by saying that "I had an advantage. I'm used to playing with my wife," but you can

always rely on Goran Ivanisevic to leap in with both feet where more timid spouses fear to tread. "I wouldn't be able to play," Goran said. "I would just want to take numbers."

It looks as though the ladies may have the last laugh. Bowing to pressure, event organizers said that they planned to introduce male models at the WTA Championship in the same city to redress the balance. Asked how she'd feel about that, Lindsay Davenport settled for a restrained "It might be nice."

Get me to the court on time

Player feels the need for speed as his trainers make a run for it

American Alex Bogomolov had a nightmare start to his match in the 2004 Pan American Games. Bogomolov's game the day before had been so gruelling that he was receiving intravenous fluid treatment to counter dehydration. But after boarding the team bus he learned that the time of his match had been brought forward, and unless he was there on time he would be disqualified.

Cue a frantic drive through the gridlocked streets of Santo Domingo in a 40-seater bus which only just got Bogomolov to the court on time … but without his trainers, which had been left behind in the hurry. Despite the fact that the pair he had to borrow from a US team official were a size too small, Bogomolov still managed to win the game.

Federer gets the horn

Roger blows them away with his outsize instrument

It's so big that he has to rest it on the ground, it'll barely fit in the luggage compartment on overseas flights and it's only been blown once. Yes, that's right – it's Roger Federer's magnificent horn or, to be more correct, the 10-foot-long wooden Alphorn that organizers of the Swiss Open presented him with in 2004 after he won his first Wimbledon title.

Showing an endearing ignorance of airline baggage allowances, let alone tennis training regimes, one of the officials remarked: "Please take it with you over the next year and practise a bit." But Federer had got off lightly. The Swiss had marked his Wimbledon triumph the year before by giving him a cow.

Andy's five-star service

The supersonic shot heard around the world

Andy Roddick won himself a place in the record books in 2004 with a serve that reached a blistering 153mph. Some said that the latest racket technology was giving the server an unfair advantage, but Roddick could have cited a historical precedent of someone who had even more help.

The word "service" probably comes from Henry VIII, who had grown too fat to throw the ball up in the air and had to get a servant to do it for him. Records list a payment to "one that served on the King's side at Tennas". It's hard to imagine anyone objecting, but then again it's hard to imagine Henry responding too well to being popped on the head by a 153mph serve.

The gruntometer

Noisy sirens wail for glory as decibel level rises

If you want to get ahead in tennis, get a grunt. The must-have accessory in the women's game was introduced in 1992 by Monica Seles, who became the unofficial Queen of the Grunters by groaning, huffing and squeaking her way to the quarter-finals at Wimbledon. A generation of young players duly took note.

Now that those players have grown up, grunting has reached epidemic level, leading the *Daily Mail* to set up its own "gruntometer" at Wimbledon in 2005. Outraged Wimbledon referee Alan Mills told the press that "grunting has got progressively worse over the years. I would really like it curbed." But Serena Williams sounded a defiant note, remarking, "I am going to carry on grunting."

The *Mail*'s gruntometer certainly recorded some impressive performances by Williams and other ladies of SW19. Defending champion Maria Sharapova grunted at 101.2 decibels, almost as loud as a police siren. But spare a thought for Elena Bovina, the rising Russian star whose grunt managed just 81 decibels – barely as much as a hairdryer.

Monarch of the game

Andy Murray scales the heights as Henman Hill falls

Play tennis for long enough, and you'll eventually have the bitter experience of being beaten by someone so young that they think Bjorn Borg was a member of Abba. And that's pretty much what happened when Andrew Murray met his idol Tim Henman in the first round of the Swiss Indoor tournament in 2005.

The game itself fell some way short of the clash of the titans that the organizers had been hoping for. The Swiss seemed oddly indifferent to this sea change in British tennis, and when the pair walked out into a half-empty arena with Queen's "I Want It All" bellowing out over the tannoy, it was clear that pathos rather than drama was going to be the order of the day.

Mistakes from Henman gifted the first set to Murray, who returned the favour by fluffing a chance to win the second and the match limped on into a deciding third set, with Murray finally edging out his opponent. Henman could be forgiven for reflecting on the passage of time and the fickleness of fate, but he could also take some comfort from the fact that he isn't the first person to have been mugged by a teenager.

Hello goodbye

Life through a lens loses its lustre

"She's a model and she's looking good," sang Kraftwerk many years ago. They could almost have been singing about Maria Sharapova, who also "poses for consumer products now and then, and for every camera gives the best she can", but the sometime model may be neglecting to give her best on court.

Seen as the next Kournikova, but with a talent for doing something other than pouting, Sharapova won Wimbledon in 2004 but has since struggled with injury. As her form dipped and she lost the No. I ranking there were signs that she was also struggling with the attention that comes with celebrity.

After her defeat in the semi-final of the 2005 Australian Open, Sharapova finally rounded on the press pack for lacking her well-developed sense of priorities, asking them to "take your pencils down, take your gruntometers down, the fashion police, put everything away and just watch the match". Pot, kettle, black?

Passions flare as Croatia triumph

Fans break out the rocketry to give the Davis Cup a colourful finish

The select club of past Davis Cup winners could scarcely be more exclusive if it had a Mayfair address, a liveried doorman and an unusually robust attitude to casual dress, which is why the news that Croatia had won the most coveted title in international tennis in 2005 was greeted with such shock.

In Davis Cup terms, Croatia were the equivalent of someone who had turned up wearing jeans, put their feet on the leather upholstery and ordered beans on toast. Where were these upstarts when the Four Musketeers first twirled their rackets, or when Don Budge turned down a $50,000 professional contract so that he could contest the Cup one last time?

The answer was "being part of Yugoslavia", but that only showed just how far Croatian tennis had come since the country had gained its independence in 1991. Croatia first competed in the Cup in 1993 and were seen as rank outsiders, but that was about to change.

Their squad for the final included Goran Ivanisevic – who didn't play, but who is always good to have along for press conferences – and,

more importantly, Mario Ancic, known as "Baby Goran". Ancic won the decisive final singles game in straight sets, giving Croatia their first Davis Cup, but it was the antics of the crowd as much as Ancic's tennis that proved to be the highlight of the evening.

Croatia's travelling support had worked hard to make their team feel at home, even though the tie was being played in Slovakia, and as Ancic won the match with his second match point they promptly went loudly, luridly mad.

A vast Croatian flag was unfurled in the stands and, with cheery disregard for health and

safety regulations, fans broke out the kind of distress flares normally reserved for the sinking of large ocean liners, and waved them overhead as though their lives depended on it. Eager to join in, the players threw their rackets into the smog, followed, inexplicably, by their shoes.

Seemingly impervious to the rioting, Ivanisevic later said that "It's easier when you are playing as you can get your emotions out properly."

Vertigo

Agassi and Federer head for the helipad as insurance premiums go through the roof

The Burj Al Arab hotel in Dubai is a testament to the idea that you should never let good taste and commonsense come between you and your dream, and it's entirely in keeping with this notion that in 2005 the hotel hosted the oddest, and potentially the most dangerous, game of tennis in history.

The 321-metre-tall, seven-star monument to vulgarity is shaped like the sail of a traditional Arab fishing boat. It has walls covered with gold leaf and bathrooms made out of the same type of marble that Michelangelo used to knock up slightly less gauche

masterpieces. To allay fears that it might ever appear understated, at night its exterior is bathed in tasteful neon pink and blue light.

Sagely understanding that the kind of people who are likely to stay in the Burj are the kind of people who like to make an entrance, the architects, who must have been wondering just how far they could go without actually making the hotel fly, did the next best thing and gave it a helipad, 200 metres up in the air.

Hearing that the Dubai Duty Free Men's Open was coming to town, someone said, presumably

as a joke, "We could publicize it by turning the Burj's helipad into a tennis court and inviting two of the world's best players to have a knock about." You don't say things like that lightly in Dubai, and soon it came to pass.

Roger Federer and Andre Agassi were the first and, to date, only players to grace the Astroturf. It made for a breathtaking spectacle, with the green of the court poised mid-air and magnificently out of context, but with a few million dollars' worth of expensive tennis

player running around with nothing between them and a messy end but prudence and a small piece of netting, it'd probably be fair to say that the players' agents were having a fraught afternoon.

They were not the only ones. Federer told the press that he had "no issues with the height as long as I didn't have to bungee jump off the side", and somewhere, above the roar of the wind going across the helipad, it may just have been possible to hear an insurance company, sobbing "Please, no more..."

100 Strawberries, cream and cash

Ringing tills are the sound of the summer as fruit sets taste-buds tingling

The essential Wimbledon delicacy, strawberries and cream have sustained many a spectator through a long tie-break on a searingly hot afternoon, as well as giving them a handy source of that all-important Vitamin C, antioxidants and potassium. The year 2005 saw the price of a portion containing at least 10 strawberries hit £2.00, but you get what you pay for.

The strawberries are Grade I Kent strawberries picked the day before and delivered to Wimbledon at 5.30 in the morning. If you find yourself at the Championships, head for Aorangi café and the Tea Lawn, both of which serve Wimbledon's favourite snack, but there's no need to hurry.

With two million individual berries and 7,000 litres of fresh cream served each year, there's enough to go round – or to reach to Reading, if they were laid end to end. Though why anyone would want to follow a trail of strawberries to Reading is rather more of a mystery.

The soldier from Limassol

Baghdatis finds that the first casualty of war is your tennis career

For a few heady days during the Australian Open, Marcos Baghdatis seemed to have it made. The unknown 20-year-old Cypriot reached the final of the tournament, but there was one opponent that the members of his camp feared more than his opponent Roger Federer – and that was the army.

Everyone in Cyprus has to do national service, normally after their 18th birthday, and it looked as though, after two short-term deferments, Baghdatis would be spending the best years of his career peeling spuds and polishing toilets with a toothbrush.

He did eventually lose to Federer in the final, but the army relented and granted him a 12-year extension. Baghdatis's girlfriend may have an opponent of her own to face – the crowd at the Open included Oscar-winning actress Charlize Theron.

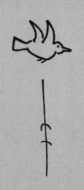

GAME, SET AND MATCH